BIBLE REFERENCE SHEETS

THE OLD TESTAMENT (KJV)

BIBLE REFERENCE SHEETS
THE OLD TESTAMENT, KJV

ISBN: 978-1-953489-24-1

Copyright ©2023 Wildrose Media. USA.

All rights reserved. No part of this publication may be reproduced, distributed or transmitted in any form or by any means without prior written permission of the publisher except in the case of brief quotations for critical reviews and certain other noncommercial uses permitted by copyright law.

YOU MAY ALSO BE INTERESTED IN:

Sermon Notebooks for Kids

Simple Sermon Notes for Kids ages 6-8
ISBN: 978-1-953489-09-8
ISBN: 978-1-953489-14-2

AVAILABLE on AMAZON

Scan the Amazon Affiliated QR Code to view book:

www.wildrose-media.com

BIBLE REFERENCE SHEETS
THE OLD TESTAMENT (KJV)

www.wildrose-media.com

GENESIS

AUTHOR: Attributed to Moses.
SETTING: Ancient Mesopotamia, the Fertile Crescent, Egypt, Syria.
TIME PERIOD: Creation to 1800 B.C. Likely written between 1445-1405 B.C.
LITERARY STYLE: Historical Narrative, Law

The OLD TESTAMENT
BOOK # 1
50 CHAPTERS

Key People
- Adam & Eve
- Cain & Abel
- Noah
- Abraham
- Lot
- Isaac
- Jacob & Esau
- Joseph
- Moses
- Pharaoh
- Aaron
- Joshua
- Melchizedek

Key Places
- Garden of Eden
- Tower of Babel
- Sodom & Gomorrah
- Egypt
- Red Sea
- Mt. Sinai/Mt. Horeb
- Canaan
- Shechem
- Hebron
- Bethel
- Jericho

Key Events
- Creation
- Sin enters the world
- Cain murders his brother Abel
- Tower of Babel
- Noah and the Flood
- Abraham & Sarah
- Sodom & Gomorrah are destroyed
- Isaac & Rebekah
- Jacob and his 12 sons
- Joseph sold by his brothers, lives in Egypt
- Famine reunites Jacob's family

KEY VERSES & NOTES

In the beginning God created the heaven and the earth.
Genesis 1:1 KJV

KEY VERSES

- 1:26-31
- 2:7
- 2:18-24
- 3:1-24
- 6:3
- 7:1
- 7:13- 8:22
- 9:1, 8-17
- 12:1-3
- 32:28
- Chapter 37
- 41:39-49
- 46:1-25
- 47:27-31
- 50:15-19

KEY WORDS
Sin
Curse
Sacrifice
Covenant

THEME
The sovereignty of God.
Redemption and reconciliation is possible by God's grace.

©2023 Wildrose Media

EXODUS

AUTHOR: Attributed to Moses (see 24:3, Mark 12:26).
SETTING: Ancient Mesopotamia, Egypt, Midian, Red Sea, Mount Sinai.
TIME PERIOD: Begins c. 1880 B.C., ends c. 1445 B.C.
LITERARY STYLE: Historical Narrative, Law

The OLD TESTAMENT
BOOK # 2
40 CHAPTERS

Key People
- The Israelites
- Moses
- Miriam
- Jethro
- Pharaoh
- Aaron
- The Priests
- Bezalel

Key Places
- Egypt
- Midian
- Nile River
- Red Sea
- Marah
- Mt. Sinai/Mt. Horeb

Key Events
- Israelites are slaves in Egypt
- Moses adopted by Pharaoh's daughter
- Moses kills a man, flees Egypt
- The Burning Bush
- Moses, Aaron, Pharaoh and the 10 Plagues
- The first Passover meal is held
- Israelites escape Egypt, cross the Red Sea
- Mt. Sinai
- The 10 Commandments and other laws given
- The Tabernacle and the Ark of the Covenant
- Dedication of the Priests
- The Golden Calf

KEY VERSES & NOTES

I am the Lord thy God, which have brought thee out of the land of Egypt, out of the house of bondage. Thou shalt have no other gods before me.
Exodus 20:2-3 KJV

KEY VERSES

- 2:23-25
- 3:2-6
- 3:14-17
- 4:29-31
- 6:6-8
- 13:8-9
- 13:21-22
- 14:29-31
- 15:2
- 20:1-17
- 23:20-22
- 28:29-30
- 34:5-7
- 40:34-38

KEY WORDS
Holy
Miracle
Covenant
Ark of the Covenant

THEME
Rescue, relationship, and redemption.

©2023 Wildrose Media

LEVITICUS

AUTHOR: Attributed to Moses.
SETTING: The Israelites are camped at the base of Mount Sinai.
TIME PERIOD: Circa 1445 B.C. Likely written between 1445-1405 B.C.
LITERARY STYLE: Historical Narrative, Law

The OLD TESTAMENT
BOOK # 3
27 CHAPTERS

Key People
- The Israelites
- Moses
- Aaron
- Nadab
- Abihu
- The Priests

Key Places
- Mt. Sinai/Mt. Horeb
- The Tabernacle

Key Events
- Instructions for sacrifices & offerings
- Ordination & consecration of the Priests
- Defining what is clean and unclean
- Laws addressing Ritual Purity
- The Day of Atonement
- Laws about holy living
- The Feast Days established
- The Sabbath and the Year of Jubilee
- Blessings for obedience, punishment for disobedience
- Redemption of people and property

KEY VERSES & NOTES

*For I am
the Lord your God:
ye shall therefore
sanctify yourselves, and
ye shall be holy;
because I am holy.*
Leviticus 11:44a KJV

KEY VERSES

- 1:2-3
- 10:10-11
- 16:34
- 17:11
- 18:4-5
- 19:2
- 20:26
- 22:3
- 23:22
- 25:10-11
- 26:3-6
- 26:14-17
- 26:38-39
- 27:30

KEY WORDS
- Holiness
- Ordination
- Offering
- Atonement

THEME
The holiness of God.
God's requirements for His chosen people.

©2023 Wildrose Media

NUMBERS

AUTHOR: Attributed to Moses (see 33:2).
SETTING: In the wilderness, the plains of Moab, & the Jordan River.
TIME PERIOD: One year after fleeing Egypt, covers period of 39 years.
LITERARY STYLE: Historical Narrative, Law

The OLD TESTAMENT
BOOK # 4
36 CHAPTERS

Key People
- The Israelites
- Moses
- Aaron
- Eleazar
- The Levites
- The Gershonites
- The Kohathites
- The Merarites
- The 70 Elders
- Korah
- The Amorites
- Balaam & Balak
- Joshua & Caleb

Key Places
- Mt. Sinai/Mt. Horeb
- Wilderness of Sinai
- Wilderness of Paran
- Wilderness of Zin
- Kadesh
- Edom
- Moab
- Canaan
- Mount Hor
- The Negev
- Hebron
- Jordan River

Key Events
- Census is taken of the Israelites
- Additional laws & duties of the Priests
- The Nazarite vow
- The Cloud of God's Presence
- Israelites set out from Mt. Sinai for Canaan
- Spies sent into Canaan, the Promised Land
- Complaints and rebellion of the people
- The budding of Aaron's staff
- Moses' strikes the rock and is punished
- The Bronze Serpent
- Travel to Moab
- Balaam's prophecies
- Joshua is chosen to lead Israel

KEY VERSES & NOTES

The Lord bless thee, and keep thee: the Lord make his face shine upon thee and be gracious unto thee: The Lord lift His countenance upon thee, and give thee peace.
Numbers 6:24-26 KJV

KEY VERSES

- 1:51-53
- 3:5-8
- 5:1-3
- 7:89
- 12:5-8
- 14:6-9:26-31
- 14:18
- 14:26-31
- 17:1-5, 8
- 21:4-9
- 23:19
- 24:17
- 27:12-14
- 27:18-20
- 30:2
- 35:6-8
- 35:34

KEY WORDS
Vow
Altar
Dedication
Anointed

THEME
There are consequences for disobedience.

©2023 Wildrose Media

DEUTERONOMY

AUTHOR: Attributed to Moses, Joshua may have written the account of Moses' death.
SETTING: The Israelites are camped east of the Jordan River.
TIME PERIOD: Events occur in a single location over a few weeks.
LITERARY STYLE: Historical Narrative, Summary, Law

The OLD TESTAMENT
BOOK # 5
34 CHAPTERS

Key People
- The Israelites
- Moses
- Joshua

Key Places
- Jordan River
- Canaan
- Plains of Moab
- Mt. Nebo
- Jericho

Key Events
- Moses addresses the second generation of Israelites who will enter the Promised Land
- Reminder of the Covenant and Law
- Rules for worship & daily living.
- Justice & the Cities of Refuge.
- Reminder of God's promised blessings for obedience, but curses for disobedience.
- Joshua becomes leader of the Israelites.
- Moses blesses Israel, then dies.

KEY VERSES & NOTES

And the Lord, he it is that doth go before thee; he will be with thee, he will not fail thee, neither forsake you: fear not, neither be dismayed.
Deuteronomy 31:8 KJV

KEY VERSES
- 1:8
- 3:21-22
- 4:1-2
- 4:20
- 4:39-40
- 5:32-33
- 6:4-5
- 7:6
- 7:9
- 8:19-20
- 10:12
- 18:22
- 28:10
- 30:19
- 31:6

KEY WORDS
- Blessings & Curses
- Worship
- Idolatry
- The Law

THEME
God's people are called to be holy, set apart from the world.

©2023 Wildrose Media

JOSHUA

AUTHOR: Attributed to Joshua, though the author is not named.
SETTING: By the Jordan River, on the plains of Moab and into Canaan.
TIME PERIOD: After the death of Moses, ends with death of Joshua.
LITERARY STYLE: Historical Narrative

The OLD TESTAMENT
BOOK # 6
24 CHAPTERS

Key People
- The Israelites
- Joshua
- Rahab
- The Spies
- Gibeonites

Key Places
- Canaan
- Jordan River
- Jericho
- Ai
- Shechem

Key Events
- Joshua takes leadership over Israel.
- Rahab protects the Spies in Jericho.
- The Israelites enter the Promised Land.
- Circumcision of Israelite males.
- The Fall of Jericho.
- Battles to conquer the land.
- The Sun stands still.
- The Gibeonites deceive Israel.
- The land is divided among the 12 tribes, with towns given to the Levites.
- Covenant renewal.
- Joshua's death and burial.
- Burial of Joseph's bones at Shechem.

KEY VERSES & NOTES

Have not I commanded thee? Be strong and of a good courage; be not afraid, neither be thou dismayed: for the LORD thy God is with thee whithersoever thou goest.
Joshua 1:9 KJV

KEY VERSES

- 1:8
- 1:9
- 6:26-27
- 10:13-14
- 11:23
- 21:43-45
- 23:6-8
- 24:14-15
- 24:32

KEY WORDS
- Consecration
- Circumcision
- Treaty
- Covenant

THEME
God is faithful. He keeps His promises.

©2023 Wildrose Media

JUDGES

AUTHOR: Attributed to Samuel, with contribution from prophets Nathan and Gad.
SETTING: The Promised land of Canaan. Before Israel had a king.
TIME PERIOD: Begins with death of Joshua, spans about 300- 450 years.
LITERARY STYLE: Historical Narrative

The OLD TESTAMENT
BOOK # 7
21 CHAPTERS

Key People
- The Israelites
- Othniel
- Ehud
- Shamgar
- Deborah
- Gideon
- Tola
- Jair
- Jepthah
- Izban
- Elon
- Abdon
- Samson

Key Places
- Canaan
- Bokim
- Jericho
- Hebron
- Mount Tabor
- Shechem
- Moab
- Valley of Jezreel
- Hill Country Ephraim
- Land of Ammon
- Dan
- Gibeah
- Mizpah

Key Events
- After Joshua's death, the Israelites have no leader.
- The Israelites disobeyed God's command to conquer the land, living among pagan nations.
- Israel abandons God, worshiping idols instead.
- God raises up a succession of leaders, Judges who warn the Israelites to turn back to God. They do for awhile then, revert to idols. This cycle of *disobedience, oppression, and deliverance* continues throughout the book.

KEY VERSES & NOTES

In those days there was no king in Israel, but every man did that which was right in his own eyes.
Judges 17:6 KJV

KEY VERSES

- 2:1-4
- 2:7
- 2:10-11
- 2:18-19
- 3:1, 3-4
- 8:22-23
- 10:11-16
- 16:28-30
- 21:25

KEY WORDS
- Apostasy
- Baal
- Ashtoreth
- Judge

THEME
God is patient and merciful, delivering His people from their enemies.

©2023 Wildrose Media

RUTH

AUTHOR: Attributed to Samuel.
SETTING: Begins in Moab, then Bethlehem in Judah. During Judges.
TIME PERIOD: During a famine at the time of the Judges.
LITERARY STYLE: Biography

The OLD TESTAMENT
BOOK # 8
4 CHAPTERS

Key People
Elimelech
Ruth
Naomi/Mara
Orpah
Boaz
Obed

Key Places
Moab
Bethlehem
Judah

Key Events
- Ephrathites Elimelech and Naomi are in Moab.
- When Naomi's husband and sons die, she decides to return to Bethlehem, in Judah.
- Ruth's daughter-in-law, Ruth goes with her.
- Ruth meets Boaz while gleaning in his field.
- Naomi's plan for the kinsman-redeemer.
- Boaz agrees to redeem Ruth.
- Boaz marries Ruth.
- The birth of Obed.
- Genealogy, the lineage of King David.

KEY VERSES & NOTES

And Ruth said, "Intreat me not to leave thee, or to return from following after thee: for whither thou goest, I will go; and where thou lodgest I will lodge: thy people shall be my people, and thy God my God."
Ruth 1:16 KJV

KEY VERSES

- 1:6
- 1:16-17
- 1:20-21
- 2:1-2
- 2:11-12
- 2:19-20
- 3:114:7
- 4:9-10
- 4:17

KEY WORDS
Kinsman-Redeemer
Glean

THEME
Ruth is a story of love and redemption, foreshadowing Christ's redemption of both Jew and Gentile.

©2023 Wildrose Media

1 SAMUEL

AUTHOR: Unknown, attributed to prophets Samuel, Nathan, and Gad.
SETTING: The land of Israel. God's people live among pagan nations.
TIME PERIOD: Over 110 years, from the last Judge to King Saul's death.
LITERARY STYLE: Historical Narrative

The OLD TESTAMENT
BOOK # 9
31 CHAPTERS

Key People
- Elkanah
- Hannah
- Samuel
- Eli
- Saul
- Jesse
- David
- Goliath
- Philistines
- Jonathan
- Abner
- Abigail

Key Places
- Hill Country Ephraim
- Ramah
- Shiloh
- Ekron
- Kiriath Jearim
- Mizpah
- Gilgal
- Carmel
- Bethlehem
- Valley of Elah
- Nob
- Witch of Endor
- Achish

Key Events
- Samuel's birth and instruction under Eli.
- Ark of the Covenant is captured & returned.
- Samuel leads the nation of Israel.
- Israel's first king, Saul.
- David is anointed king by Samuel.
- David slays Goliath, victory over Philistines.
- David lives in Saul's court, his friendship with Jonathan.
- David flees from Saul who wishes to kill him.
- David, Nabal, and Abigail.
- Saul consults a witch.
- Battles against pagan nations.
- King Saul's death.

KEY VERSES & NOTES

For man looketh on the outward appearance, but the Lord looketh on the heart.
1 Samuel 16:7b KJV

KEY VERSES

- 1:11
- 1:27-28
- 2:2
- 2:10
- 2:26
- 8:6-9
- 10:1, 6-7
- 12:24-25
- 15:26-29, 35
- 16:13-14
- 24:12,13
- 28:15-19
- 29:5
- 30:6

KEY WORDS
Prophet
Vow
Anoint
High Place

THEME
God humbles the proud and exalts the humble.
"It is not by strength that one prevails" (vs. 9b).

©2023 Wildrose Media

2 SAMUEL

AUTHOR: Unknown, attributed to prophets Samuel, Nathan, and Gad.
SETTING: The land of Israel. God's people live among pagan nations.
TIME PERIOD: From Saul's death c. 1011 B.C. through Davids 40-year reign.
LITERARY STYLE: Historical Narrative

The OLD TESTAMENT
BOOK # 10
24 CHAPTERS

Key People
- David
- Abner
- Ish-Bosheth
- Joab
- Michal
- Jebusites
- Nathan
- Mephibosheth
- Bathsheba
- Uriah
- Solomon
- Absalom
- Gad

Key Places
- Ziklag
- Hebron
- Gibeon
- Jerusalem
- Jordan River
- Israel
- Judah

Key Events
- David mourns for Saul and Jonathan
- David is king over Judah
- Battles between Judah and Israel
- David is king over Israel, uniting the nation
- Jerusalem conquered, becomes capital city
- God establishes a covenant with David
- Wars with pagan nations
- David's adultery, Uriah's death
- Absalom's rebellion and death
- David's song of praise
- List of David's mighty men
- Plague in Israel and God's forgiveness

KEY VERSES & NOTES

As for God, his way is perfect; the word of the Lord is tried: he is a buckler to all them that trust in Him.
2 Samuel 22:31 KJV

KEY VERSES

- 1:11-12
- 3:1
- 5:1-3
- 5:9-10
- 7:12-16
- 8:15
- 12:11-13
- 21:13-14
- 22:2-4
- 22:47-51
- 24:10, 17
- 24:25

KEY WORDS
Davidic Covenant

THEME
God's sovereignty and sin's consequences.

©2023 Wildrose Media

1 KINGS

AUTHOR: Unknown, may have been Ezra, Isaiah, or Jeremiah.
SETTING: In the ancient kingdoms of Israel and Judah.
TIME PERIOD: History of the kings from about 970 B.C. to 852 B.C.
LITERARY STYLE: Historical Narrative, Chronicle

The OLD TESTAMENT
BOOK # 11
22 CHAPTERS

Key People
- David
- Adonijah
- Solomon
- Joab
- Abiathar
- Zadok
- Nathan
- Hiram king of Tyre
- Ahab & Jezebel
- Elijah
- Elisha
- Naboth

Key Places
- Judah
- Israel
- Gibeon
- Jerusalem
- Shechem
- Bethel
- Mount Carmel
- Samaria
- Ramoth Gilead

Key Events
- Adonijah attempts to become king
- Solomon becomes king
- David's death
- Solomon's wealth & wisdom
- Solomon builds the Temple
- Dedication of the Temple
- Death of Solomon, Rehoboam becomes king
- The Kingdom divides
- The first kings of Judah and Israel
- Shrines, altars, and worship of pagan gods
- Elijah and the prophets of Baal
- Elisha is called to help Elijah
- Israel and Judah join forces, death of Ahab

KEY VERSES & NOTES

And he said, LORD God of Israel, there is no God like thee, in heaven above, or on earth beneath, who keepest covenant and mercy with thy servants that walk before thee with all their heart.
1 Kings 8:23 KJV

KEY VERSES

- 1:29-30
- 2:2-4
- 2:31-33
- 3:5-14
- 4:29-34
- 6:1
- 8:10-14
- 9:3-9
- 11:9-12
- 11:34-36
- 12:20-24
- 18:36-39
- 21:25-29

KEY WORDS
Prophet
Wisdom
Discernment

THEME
God's word is true.
God rewards faithfulness and punishes disobedience.

©2023 Wildrose Media

2 KINGS

AUTHOR: Unknown, may have been Ezra, Isaiah, or Jeremiah.
SETTING: In the kingdoms of Israel and Judah.
TIME PERIOD: Events occur between c. 852 B.C. to 561 B.C.
LITERARY STYLE: Historical Narrative, a Chronicle.

The OLD TESTAMENT
BOOK # 12
25 CHAPTERS

Key People
- Elijah
- Elisha
- Joram
- Jehosophat
- The Widow
- Naaman
- Jehu
- Ahaz
- Isaiah
- Sennacherib
- Hezekiah
- Josiah
- Nebuchadnezzar

Key Places
- Samaria
- Jordan River
- Bethel
- Jerusalem
- Assyria
- Israel
- Judah
- Babylon

Key Events
- Elijah is taken up to heaven
- Elisha & miracles in the Northern Kingdom
  - the widow's oil, boy restored to life
  - axehead floats
- A history of the Kings of Israel and Judah.
- The exile of Israel (Northern Kingdom)
- King Hezekiah
- King Josiah has the Temple repaired, finds the Book of the Law and renews the covenant
- Babylonians attack the kingdom of Judah
- Judah is taken captive

KEY VERSES & NOTES

And it came to pass, as they still went on, and talked, that, behold, there appeared a chariot of fire, and horses of fire, and parted them both asunder; and Elijah went up by a whirlwind into heaven.
2 Kings 2:11 KJV

KEY VERSES

- 2:11, 15
- 4:1-7
- 6:15-17
- 8:11-13
- 8:16-19
- 12:1-5
- 17:5-8
- 18:1-5
- 23:1-3
- 23:26-27
- 24:20
- 25:8-12

KEY WORDS
Captivity

THEME
Rebellion against God results in punishment.

©2023 Wildrose Media

1 CHRONICLES

AUTHOR: Unknown, attributed to Ezra in Jewish tradition.
SETTING: Israel is in Babylonian captivity, some exiles have returned.
TIME PERIOD: A review of God's people, from Adam to King David.
LITERARY STYLE: Historical Narrative

The OLD TESTAMENT
BOOK # 13
29 CHAPTERS

Key People
- Japhethites
- Hamites
- Semites
- Abraham
- 12 Tribes of Israel
- Aaron
- Edomites
- Philistines
- Ammonites
- Saul
- David
- Solomon
- The Levites

Key Places
- Israel
- Judah
- Kireath-Jiram
- Jerusalem

Key Events
- Genealogy from Adam to Saul.
- The death of King Saul.
- King David.
- God's covenant with King David.
- Wars with pagan nations.
- The Temple and the Priesthood.
- Israel's army.
- Plans for the Temple.
- Solomon becomes king.
- Death of King David.

KEY VERSES & NOTES

O give thanks unto the Lord; for he is good; for his mercy endureth forever.
1 Chronicles 16:34 KJV

KEY VERSES
- 10:13-14
- 16:8
- 16:22
- 17:14
- 17:20-22
- 22:6-10
- 22:19
- 28:20
- 29:14
- 29:18-20

KEY WORDS
Chronicle

THEME
A reminder to be faithful to God and His covenant. God is faithful.

©2023 Wildrose Media

2 CHRONICLES

AUTHOR: Unknown, Jewish tradition attributes it to Ezra.
SETTING: The Southern Kingdom of Judah, to Babylon and exile.
TIME PERIOD: From King Solomon to King Cyrus, c. 971 B.C. to 538 B.C.
LITERARY STYLE: Historical Narrative, a Chronicle of Events.

The OLD TESTAMENT
BOOK # 14
36 CHAPTERS

Key People
- Solomon
- Queen of Sheba
- Rehoboam
- Abijah
- Asa
- Jehoshaphat
- Ahab
- Elijah
- Jehoiada
- Ahaz
- Hezekiah
- Josiah
- Cyrus of Persia

Key Places
- Jerusalem
- Tyre
- Mount Moriah
- Israel
- Judah

Key Events
- The reign of King Solomon.
- Solomon builds the temple.
- Description of the Temple.
- The nation of Israel is divided in two Kingdoms, Northern and Southern.
- The kings of Judah (the Southern Kingdom).
- The fall of Jerusalem and Judah's exile.
- King Cyrus of Persia permits Jews to return to Jerusalem and rebuild the Temple.

KEY VERSES & NOTES

But they mocked the messengers of God, and despised his words, and misused his prophets until the wrath of the Lord arose against his people, till there was no remedy.
2 Chronicles 36:16 KJV

KEY VERSES

- 1:8-12
- 2:5
- 5:13-6:2
- 6:14-17
- 7:1-3
- 7:14
- 11:13-17
- 13:12
- 19:6,9
- 20:21-22
- 21:29
- 24:20
- 28:24-25
- 30:6-13
- 33:10-12,16
- 36:15-19
- 36:22-23

KEY WORDS
Most Holy Place
Ark of the Covenant
Exile

THEME
Restoration.
God is a God of love and forgiveness.

©2023 Wildrose Media

EZRA

AUTHOR: Attributed to Ezra.
SETTING: Begins in Babylon, ends in Jerusalem in Judah.
TIME PERIOD: Between 539 B.C. and 458 B.C.
LITERARY STYLE: Historical Narrative

The OLD TESTAMENT
BOOK # 15
10 CHAPTERS

Key People
- Cyrus
- Sheshbazzar
- Darius
- The Levites
- Nehemiah
- Zerubbabel
- Artaxerxes
- Haggai
- Zechariah
- Ezra

Key Places
- Persia
- Jerusalem
- Babylon

Key Events
- The return of the first Babylonian (now Persian) exiles to Jerusalem.
- Rebuilding of the altar and the Temple.
- Interference by other nations.
- Decree of Darius read.
- Ezra returns to Jerusalem.
- The Jews confess their sins.
- Intermarriage is addressed by Ezra.

KEY VERSES & NOTES

The hand of our God is upon all them for good that seek him; but his power and his wrath is against all them that forsake him.
Ezra 8:22b KJV

KEY VERSES

- 1:1-3
- 1:7
- 2:68-70
- 3:10-13
- 4:4-5
- 6:21-22
- 7:1,6,10
- 7:13, 25-26
- 8:21-23
- 8:28-30
- 10:2-3
- 10:16-17

KEY WORDS
Covenant

THEME
God's grace and continuing covenant with Israel.

©2023 Wildrose Media

NEHEMIAH

AUTHOR: Attributed to Ezra.
SETTING: Begins in Babylon, ends in Jerusalem in Judah.
TIME PERIOD: Between 539 B.C. and 458 B.C.
LITERARY STYLE: Historical Narrative

The OLD TESTAMENT
BOOK # 16
13 CHAPTERS

Key People
- Nehemiah
- Artaxerxes

Key Places
- Susa
- Jerusalem
- Judah

Key Events
- Nehemiah hears of Jerusalem's troubles and prays
- Nehemiah returns to Jerusalem to rebuild the walls
- Opposition to the rebuilding
- The wall and gates of Jerusalem are completed
- The people who returned to Judah are registered
- Renewal of the Covenant
- Confession of sins
- The Feast of Tabernacles
- Nehemiah returns to Persia
- The wall is dedicated
- Nehemiah returns to Jerusalem for a second term as governor
- Nehemiah rebukes and corrects the Israelites

KEY VERSES & NOTES

Then I answered them, and said unto them, "the God of heaven, he will prosper us; therefore we his servants will arise and build..."
Nehemiah 2:20a KJV

KEY VERSES

- 1:3-7
- 2:17-18
- 4:14
- 5:9-13
- 5:14
- 5:19
- 6:15-16
- 8:2-3, 6
- 9:5b-6
- 9:32-33

KEY WORDS
Remnant
Cupbearer
The Law
Covenant

THEME
Restoration.
God's covenant faithfulness to Israel.

©2023 Wildrose Media

ESTHER

AUTHOR: Unknown but familiar with Jewish and Persian customs & feasts.
SETTING: Susa, Persia c. 25 years before Ezra returns to Jerusalem.
TIME PERIOD: Between 483 B.C. and 473 B.C.
LITERARY STYLE: Biography

The OLD TESTAMENT
BOOK # 17
10 CHAPTERS

Key People
King Xerxes
Queen Vashti
Mordecai
Hadassah/Esther
Haman

Key Places
Susa
Persia

Key Events
- Queen Vashti is deposed at the King's banquet
- Esther becomes Queen
- Haman's plot to destroy the Jews
- Mordecai asks Esther for help
- Haman is executed
- Victory for the Jews
- Purim is celebrated

KEY VERSES & NOTES

Then Queen Esther answered, "If I have found favor in thy sight, O king, and if it please the king, let my life be given me at my petition, and my people at my request".
Esther 7:3 KJV

KEY VERSES

- 1:10, 12
- 2:1-4
- 2:7-10
- 2:17
- 3:5-11
- 4:15-16
- 7:1-10
- 8:11
- 9:27-28

KEY WORDS
Edict
Purim

THEME
God is faithful, he preserves His people.

©2023 Wildrose Media

JOB

AUTHOR: Unknown, attributed to Moses.
SETTING: Job lived in the land of Uz.
TIME PERIOD: Seems to have occurred after Babel but before Abraham.
LITERARY STYLE: Poetry, Wisdom Literature

The OLD TESTAMENT
BOOK # 18
42 CHAPTERS

Key People
Job
The Chaldeans
Eliphaz
Bildad
Zophar

Key Places
Uz

Key Events
- Introduction to Job
- Satan approaches God in heaven
- Job's first test
- Job's second test
- Dialogue between Job and his three friends
- God speaks to Job
- God rebukes Job's friends
- God blesses Job

KEY VERSES & NOTES

"All the while my breath is in me, and the Spirit of God is in my nostrils; my lips shall not speak wickedness, nor my tongue utter deceit."
Job 27:3-4 KJV

KEY VERSES

- 1:8
- 1:12
- 1:20-21
- 2:9-10
- 5:17
- 11:7
- 12:10, 13, 16
- 19:25-27
- 23:13-14
- 27:3-4
- 42:1-6
- 42:10

KEY WORDS
Fear God
Satan – accuser
Righteous

THEME
God as the authority over all, trust Him despite our circumstances.

©2023 Wildrose Media

THE BOOK of PSALMS

AUTHOR: David, Solomon, sons of Asaph & Korah, Moses, two Ezrahite brothers.
SETTING: Ancient Mesopotamia and Israel.
TIME PERIOD: Difficult to date but likely between 1500 B.C. and 500 B.C.
LITERARY STYLE: Poetry, Songs of Praise, Wisdom

The OLD TESTAMENT
BOOK # 19
150 PSALMS

Key People
- David
- Solomon
- Asaph
- Korah
- Moses
- Ethan
- Heman

Key Places
- Jerusalem
- Zion/ Mount Zion
- Judah
- Israel
- The Heavens

Key Events
- There are several themes or types of Psalms.
- Some Psalms may fit into more than one theme/category.
- Historical Psalms – God's acts and Israel's response
- Psalms of Praise and Adoration to God
- Psalms of Lament
- Psalms of Thanksgiving
- Liturgical Psalms – worship, used during Feasts
- Imprecatory/Petition – call on God for help
- Relational Psalms – between God and writer
- Prophetic Psalms – the coming Messiah

KEY VERSES & NOTES

Let the words of my mouth, and the meditation of my heart, be acceptable in thy sight, O LORD, my strength, and my redeemer.
Psalm 19:14 KJV

KEY VERSES

- Psalm 1
- Psalm 8
- Psalm 14:1
- Psalm 15
- Psalm 19
- Psalm 23
- Psalm 27:4
- Psalm 46:1
- Psalm 51:10
- Psalm 55
- Psalm 62
- Psalm 91
- Psalm 96
- Psalm 100
- Psalm 103
- Psalm 119:105
- Psalm 121
- Psalm 139

KEY WORDS
Psalm – Tehilim - Mizmôr
Selah

THEME
God is the sovereign center of life, history and the universe. He deserves our worship.

©2023 Wildrose Media

PROVERBS

AUTHOR: Known authors are Solomon, Hezekiah, Lemuel & Agur.
SETTING: Written by kings of ancient Israel/Judah.
TIME PERIOD: Solomon ruled 971-931 B.C., Hezekiah from c. 715-686 B.C.
LITERARY STYLE: Poetry, Wisdom Literature

The OLD TESTAMENT
BOOK # 20
31 CHAPTERS

Key People

Generalizations:
- Men
- Young Men
- Son
- Father
- Woman
- A Wife
- Servant
- The Wicked
- The Fool

Key Places

Key Events

- A proverb is a figure of speech which allows a person to express complex ideas in a compact statement. It is often culturally or traditionally based and may be down passed from generation to generation.
- Proverbs often educate or offer advice, wisdom, and moral truths.
- There is no plot or storyline in the book of Proverbs.
- It is a collection of sayings which address many opposing topics, including wisdom and foolishness, joy vs. anger, diligence vs. laziness, justice vs. injustice, what God loves vs. what He hates.

KEY VERSES & NOTES

*"The fear of the LORD
is the beginning
of knowledge:
but fools despise
wisdom and instruction."*
Proverbs 1:7 KJV

KEY VERSES

- 1:32-33
- 3:5-6
- 6:16-19
- 8:36
- 9:10
- 10:11
- 13:1, 3
- 14:16, 31
- 15:1, 28
- 18:12, 21
- 21:3
- 26:28
- 28:6
- 29:23
- 31:10-31

KEY WORDS

Proverb
Wisdom
Discernment

THEME

True wisdom comes from God.

©2023 Wildrose Media

ECCLESIASTES

AUTHOR: The author refers to himself as a teacher. May have been Solomon.
SETTING: The nation of Israel.
TIME PERIOD: None mentioned, Solomon reigned 970 B.C. to 931 B.C.
LITERARY STYLE: Poetry, Wisdom Literature

The OLD TESTAMENT
BOOK # 21
12 CHAPTERS

Key People
The Teacher
Generalizations:
- Man
- Woman
- The King

Key Places

Key Events
- Preface
- Introduction
- Seeking Meaning Through Pleasure
- Seeking Meaning Through Wisdom and Folly
- Seeking Wisdom Through Work and Rewards
- Conclusions - Man's Limitations and Human Mortality
- Words of Advice
- Information about the Author

KEY VERSES & NOTES

Fear God, and keep his commandments: for this is the whole duty of man. For God shall bring every work into judgment, with every secret thing whether it be good or whether it be evil.
Ecclesiastes 12:13b-14 KJV

KEY VERSES

- 1:2, 8-11
- 1:18
- 2:12-14
- 3:1-8
- 3:14
- 4:9-12
- 5:5
- 5:12
- 5:19
- 7:14
- 11:5
- 12:13-14

KEY WORDS
Meaningless
Fool/Folly
Wisdom

THEME
Without God life is meaningless.

©2023 Wildrose Media

SONG of SOLOMON

AUTHOR: A love poem between Solomon and a Shulamite woman.
SETTING: The nation of Israel, during King Solomon's reign.
TIME PERIOD: Between 971 B.C. and 931 B.C.
LITERARY STYLE: Poetry

The OLD TESTAMENT
BOOK # 22
8 CHAPTERS

Key People
Beloved
Friends
Lover
Solomon

Key Places
The King's Chambers
Jerusalem

Key Events
- Courtship and Expression of Longing
- Praise of the Beloved
- Praises of the Bride
- Disappearance of the Lover
- The Lovers are Reunited

KEY VERSES & NOTES

*I am my beloved's,
and his desire
is towards me.*
Song of Songs 7:10 KJV

KEY VERSES

- 1:2
- 1:15-16
- 2:2
- 2:5
- 2:12
- 2:16
- 3:4-5
- 4:9
- 5:8
- 7:9
- 7:12
- 8:6

KEY WORDS
Beloved

THEME
A celebration of God-ordained intimacy between man and wife.

ISAIAH

AUTHOR: The prophet Isaiah.
SETTING: The southern kingdom of Judah, in and around Jerusalem.
TIME PERIOD: Isaiah's ministry, between c. 739 B.C. and 686 B.C.
LITERARY STYLE: Prose, Poetry, Prophecy

The OLD TESTAMENT
BOOK # 23
66 CHAPTERS

Key People
- Messiah
- Jesse
- The Remnant
- Israel/Jacob
- Isaiah
- Hezekiah

Key Places
- Jerusalem
- Judah
- Zion
- Assyria
- Babylon
- Moab
- Damascus
- Cush
- Egypt
- Edom
- Tyre

Key Events
CHAPTERS 1-35
   Messages of Judgment Against Judah
   • A Call to Repentance and Holiness
   • Promised Restoration
CHAPTERS 36-39
   Isaiah's Ministry to Hezekiah
CHAPTERS 40-66
   Messages of Forgiveness, Comfort, Hope, and Salvation
   • The Future Messiah
   • The Future Kingdom

KEY VERSES & NOTES

Behold, God is my salvation; I will trust, and not be afraid: for the LORD JEHOVAH is my strength and my song; he also is become my salvation.
Isaiah 12:2 KJV

KEY VERSES

- 1:16-20
- Ch. 6
- 7:14
- 9:2-7
- Ch. 11
- 12:2
- 14:12-15
- Ch. 24
- Ch. 26+27
- Ch. 34+35
- Ch. 40
- 41:10
- 45:7
- Ch. 53
- 54:17
- 55:6-9
- 55:6-9
- 57:1-2
- 60:1
- 64:6, 8-9
- Ch. 65+66

KEY WORDS
The Day of the Lord
Judgment
Remnant
Restoration
The Holy One of Israel

THEME
God's plan for the world, and He is the source of salvation.

©2023 Wildrose Media

JEREMIAH

AUTHOR: Jeremiah the prophet. Baruch and Seraiah wrote his words down.
SETTING: During reign of Josiah, Jehoiakim, Jehoiachin, & Zedekiah.
TIME PERIOD: Jeremiah served as prophet from c.627 B.C. - 586 B.C.
LITERARY STYLE: Anthology, Prophecy, Poetry

The OLD TESTAMENT
BOOK # 24
52 CHAPTERS

Key People
- Jeremiah
- Nation of Israel
- Pashhur
- Zedekiah
- Hezekiah
- Josiah
- Jehoiachin
- Jehoiakim
- House of David
- Nebuchadnezzar
- Baruch
- Ebed-Melech
- Johanan

Key Places
- Judah
- Jerusalem
- Kings of the north
- Shiloh
- Topeth
- Perath
- Babylon
- Egypt
- Philistines
- Moab
- Ammon
- Edom
- Elam

Key Events
CHAPTER 1-29
- God's call to Jeremiah and Jeremiah's prophecies against Judah
- God pronounces judgment on Judah for idolatry, breaking the covenant.

CHAPTER 7-10 The Temple Sermon
CHAPTER 25 God's wrath extends to all nations
CHAPTER 30-33 Restoration and the New Covenant
CHAPTER 46-49 Prophesies of judgment against the nations
CHAPTER 50-51 The Babylonians, having been used by God to punish Israel, must now pay for their wickedness
CHAPTER 34-39, 52 The Fall of Jerusalem

KEY VERSES & NOTES

But this shall be the covenant that I will make with the house of Israel; After those days, saith the LORD, I will put my law in their inward parts, and write it in their hearts; and will be their God, and they shall be my people.
Jeremiah 31:33, KJV

KEY VERSES

- 1:9-10, 14
- 5:14-18
- 9:23-24
- 13:11
- 16:14-15
- 22:8-9
- 23:5-6, 20
- 26:16-19
- 31:29-30
- 31:31-34
- 33: 14-22
- 46:28
- 51:47-49
- Chapter 52

KEY WORDS

Sovereign Lord
Unfaithful/Faithless
Forsaken
Perish
New Covenant
Restoration

THEME

Judgment and hope.
God punishes sin, but remains steadfast and faithful.

©2023 Wildrose Media

LAMENTATIONS

AUTHOR: Attributed to Jeremiah, the "weeping prophet".
SETTING: Possibly after Jeremiah travels from Egypt to Babylon.
TIME PERIOD: After the destruction of Jerusalem in 586 B.C.
LITERARY STYLE: Poetry, the title means "funeral songs", sorrow & mourning

The OLD TESTAMENT
BOOK # 25
5 CHAPTERS

Key People
Daughter of Zion
Sons of Zion

Key Places
Judah
Jerusalem

Key Events
Consists of five poems, one per chapter.
1 Jerusalem's Destruction
2 God's Anger and Punishment
3 Jeremiah's Grief, a Personal Experience
4 God's Wrath
5 Prayer for God's Mercy

KEY VERSES & NOTES

*Turn thou us
unto thee, O Lord,
and we shall be turned;
renew our days as of old.*
Lamentations 5:21 KJV

KEY VERSES

- 1:1, 5
- 1:8
- 2:17
- 3:19-26
- 3:31-33
- 3:37-39
- 4:22
- 5:15-16
- 5:19-21

KEY WORDS
Mourn
Affliction
Rejected
Fulfilled
Salvation

THEME
God is faithful, merciful, and just.
He fulfills His covenant promises.
God rewards the faithful and disciplines the unfaithful.

©2023 Wildrose Media

EZEKIEL

AUTHOR: The prophet Ezekiel, who was from a priestly family.
SETTING: Ezekiel ministers to the exiles in Babylon- the Jews in Judea.
TIME PERIOD: Begins c. 593 B.C. 5 years after the exile, continues 22 years later.
LITERARY STYLE: Allegory, Parables, History, Prophecy

The OLD TESTAMENT
BOOK # 26
48 CHAPTERS

Key People
Isaiah
House of Israel
The elders
"Countrymen"
The Priests

Key Places
Jerusalem
Babylon
Samaria
Assyrians
Ammon
Moab
Edom
Philistia
Tyre
Egypt
Lebanon
Magog
The Temple

Key Events
CHAPTERS 1-3 Ezekiel's Commission
CHAPTERS 4-24 God's Judgment on Jerusalem & Judah
CHAPTERS 8-11 Temple Vision
God's Glory Departs
CHAPTERS 25-32
Oracles of God's Judgment Against Foreign Nations
CHAPTER 33 The Fall of Jerusalem & Captivity
CHAPTER 37 The Valley of Dry Bones
CHAPTERS 33-40 Future Blessings
The Restoration of Israel & Judah
CHAPTERS 40-46 Israel and the New Temple

KEY VERSES & NOTES

A new heart also will I give you, and a new spirit will I put within you: and I will take away the stony heart out of your flesh, and I will give you a heart of flesh.
Ezekiel 36:26, KJV

KEY VERSES

- 2:1-7
- 3:10-11
- 5:5-8
- 5:11-15
- 6:8-10
- 11:16-21
- 12:28
- 16:59-60
- 18:1-4, 20
- 18:30-32
- 34:17, 22-31
- 36:22-27
- 37:1-14
- 37:26-28
- 39:21-22
- 43:7
- 44:15-16
- 47:21-23

KEY WORDS
Allegory
Oracle / Vision
The Sovereign Lord
Idolatry
Covenant

THEME
God's sovereignty.
He is holy and must be honored

©2023 Wildrose Media

DANIEL

AUTHOR: Daniel, a Jew brought to Babylon by King Nebuchadnezzar.
SETTING: In Babylon.
TIME PERIOD: Between 605 B.C. and 535 B.C., during Judah's captivity.
LITERARY STYLE: History, Prophecy

The OLD TESTAMENT
BOOK # 27
12 CHAPTERS

Key People
- Daniel
- Hananiah
- Mishael
- Azariah
- Nebuchadnezzar
- The Astrologers
- Arioch
- Captive Jews
- Darius

Key Places
- Babylon
- Jerusalem
- Media
- Persia
- The North
- The South
- Egypt
- Ammon
- Edom
- Moab

Key Events
- Ch. 1 Daniel and his friends are faithful in captivity.
- Ch. 2 Nebuchadnezzar II Dreams of a Statue, Daniel interprets it.
- Ch. 3 The Fiery Furnace
- Ch. 4 Nebuchadnezzar II's Dream of the Tall Tree, Daniel interprets it.
- Ch. 5 The Writing on the Wall, Daniels interpretation. Darius becomes king over Babylon.
- Ch. 6 Daniel in the Lion's Den
- Ch. 7 & 8 Daniel's Visions: Four Beasts, the Antichrist, and Tribulation.
- Ch. 9 Daniel's Prayer, Prophecy of the 70 Weeks
- Ch. 10-12 Vision of the Future: End Times, the Kings of the North and South.

KEY VERSES & NOTES

"... for he is the living God, and stedfast for ever, and his kingdom that which shall not be destroyed, and his dominion shall be even unto the end".
Daniel 6:27b KJV

KEY VERSES
- 2:19-23
- 2:27-30
- 2:31-49
- 3:17-30
- 3:34
- 4:37
- 5:21
- 6:25-27
- 7:13-14
- 7:23-27
- 8:13-14
- 9:17-27
- 10:10-14
- 11:40-45
- 12:1-2, 9-12

KEY WORDS
- Vision
- Interpret
- Kingdom
- Decree
- Seventy 7's/Weeks
- Judgment

THEME
Hope for Israel's future.
God's sovereignty over all nations.

©2023 Wildrose Media

HOSEA

AUTHOR: Written by Hosea, one of the 12 minor prophets.
SETTING: The Southern (Judah) & Northern (Ephraim) Kingdoms.
TIME PERIOD: Between c. 755-715 B.C. During lifetime of Micah & Isaiah.
LITERARY STYLE: Poetry, Prose, History & Prophecy

The OLD TESTAMENT
BOOK # 28
14 CHAPTERS

Key People
- Hosea
- Gomer
- Israel/Jacob

Key Places
- Israel
- Judah
- Ephraim
- Benjamin
- Egypt
- Assyria
- Samaria

Key Events
- Hosea's Marriage to the prostitute Gomer
- Birth and Naming of their Children
- Israel's Sin
- Hosea's Message for Israel
- God's Discipline
- God's Merciful Restoration

KEY VERSES & NOTES

...for the ways of the Lord are right; and the just shall walk in them: but the transgressors shall fall therein.
Hosea 14:9b KJV

KEY VERSES

- 2:8
- 2:18-20
- 3:1
- 3:4
- 4:1
- 5:14-15
- 6:1
- 6:6
- 7:13-15
- 9:1-3
- 9:17
- 12:6
- 13:4-5

KEY WORDS
- Adulterous / Unfaithful
- Unrepentant
- Rebuke
- Justice
- Restoration
- Compassion

THEME
God's enduring love and faithfulness to His people, despite their idolatry.

©2023 Wildrose Media

JOEL

AUTHOR: The prophet Joel (1:1). Book two of the minor prophets.
SETTING: The Southern Kingdom of Judah, likely during Joash's reign.
TIME PERIOD: C. 835- 796 B.C., about 250 years before the Babylonian exile.
LITERARY STYLE: Poetry, Prophecy

The OLD TESTAMENT
BOOK # 29
3 CHAPTERS

Key People
Joel
Elders
Priests

Key Places
Zion
Mount Zion
Jerusalem
Judah
Valley of Jehoshaphat

Key Events
- A Plague of Locusts (either real or symbolic)
- A Call for Repentance
- The Day of the Lord
- A Call for Repentance
- The Lord's Final Judgment on the Nations
- Restoration and Blessings for God's People

KEY VERSES & NOTES

And rend your heart, and not your garments, and turn unto the LORD your God: for he is gracious and merciful, slow to anger, and of great kindness, and repenteth him of the evil.
Joel 2:13 KJV

KEY VERSES

- 1:15
- 2:1-2
- 2:11-13
- 2:18
- 2:27
- 2:28-32
- 3:17, 20-21

KEY WORDS
Mourn
Jealous
The Great and Dreadful Day of the Lord
Deliverance

THEME
Be prepared, the Day of the Lord is near.

©2023 Wildrose Media

AMOS

AUTHOR: Amos, a shepherd from a village south of Jerusalem (7:14-15).
SETTING: The Northern Kingdom of Israel.
TIME PERIOD: During reign of Jereboam II, a time of wealth & prosperity.
LITERARY STYLE: Narrative, Exhortation, Poetry

The OLD TESTAMENT
BOOK # 30
9 CHAPTERS

Key People
- Amos
- Israel/Jacob
- Nazarites
- Amaziah
- Jereboam
- David

Key Places
- Jerusalem
- Damascus
- Philistia
- Tyre
- Edom
- Ammon
- Moab
- Judah
- Israel
- Egypt

Key Events
- God's Judgment Upon Israel's Enemies (Syria, Philistia, Tyre, Edom, Ammon, and Moab)
- Judgment on Israel and Judah
- Israel's Sin, Guilt, and Punishment
- Five Visions of Judgment
- Restoration of Israel

KEY VERSES & NOTES

Seek good, and not evil, that ye may live: and so the LORD, the God of hosts shall be with you, as ye have spoken.
Amos 5:14a KJV

KEY VERSES

- 2:4-5
- 3:1-2
- 3:7
- 3:1-2
- 4:12-13
- 5:4
- 5:14-15
- 5:24
- 7:7-8
- 8:11
- 8:11-14
- 9:11, 14-15

KEY WORDS
I Will Send Fire...
Hear This...
Woe to You...
The Sovereign Lord
Deliver

THEME
Neither Jew nor Gentile is immune from God's judgment.

©2023 Wildrose Media

OBADIAH

AUTHOR: The prophet Obadiah.
SETTING: Written following an attack on Jerusalem.
TIME PERIOD: It is thought Obadiah was a contemporary of Elijah & Elisha.
LITERARY STYLE: Prophecy

The OLD TESTAMENT
BOOK # 31
1 CHAPTER

Key People
"The Nations"
Esau/Edomites

Key Places
Edom/Esau
Jerusalem
Philistia
Ephraim
Samaria
Benjamin
Gilead
The Negev

Key Events
- God judges Edom, who had not assisted the kingdom of Judah when it was attacked. (the Edomites were descendants of Esau, Jacobs' twin brother)
- Edom's Punishment
- The Restoration of Israel

KEY VERSES & NOTES

*For the day of the Lord
is near upon all heathen:
as thou hast done, it shall be
done unto thee;
thy reward shall return upon
thine own head.*
Obadiah 1:15 KJV

KEY VERSES

- Verse 3 & 4
- Verse 12
- Verse 15
- Verse 17

KEY WORDS
Destruction
Disaster
Deliver

THEME
What you sow, you will reap.
God will punish those who harm His people.

©2023 Wildrose Media

JONAH

AUTHOR: Attributed to Jonah who was from the Northern Kingdom.
SETTING: From Israel, to Joppa, to Nineveh (the capital of Assyria).
TIME PERIOD: Reign of Jereboam, king of Israel from 793 B.C.-753 B.C.
LITERARY STYLE: Historical Narrative, Poetry

The OLD TESTAMENT
BOOK # 32
4 CHAPTERS

Key People
- Jonah
- Captain & Sailors
- The Ninevites

Key Places
- Israel
- Joppa
- Ship bound for Spain
- Inside a Great Fish
- Nineveh

Key Events
- God Tells Jonah to Warn Nineveh of Coming Destruction
- Jonah Flees from His Calling
- Storm at Sea
- Jonah is Thrown Overboard and is Swallowed by a Great Fish
- Jonah Submits to God and is Vomited onto Dry Land
- Jonah goes to Nineveh
- The Ninevites Repent & Avoid Destruction
- Jonah Questions God's Mercy
- God Rebukes Jonah

KEY VERSES & NOTES

Salvation is of the Lord.
Jonah 2:9b KJV

KEY VERSES

- 1:9
- 1:11-17
- 2:1-2
- 2:8-9
- 3:3-5
- 3:10
- 4:1-2
- 4:4

KEY WORDS
Great Fish
3 Days and 3 Nights
Proclaim

THEME
God's love and mercy extends to Gentiles as well as Jews.

©2023 Wildrose Media

MICAH

AUTHOR: Micah (1:1).
SETTING: Micah ministered in Jerusalem, Judah & Samaria.
TIME PERIOD: C. 735 B.C.-700 B.C., same time period as Isaiah, Amos & Hosea
LITERARY STYLE: Prophecy

The OLD TESTAMENT
BOOK # 33
7 CHAPTERS

Key People
Leaders
Rulers
Prophets
Israel/Jacob
Remnant of Jacob

Key Places
Samaria
Jerusalem
The Temple Hill
Bethlehem
Assyria

Key Events
About Micah:
- Proclaims the Assyrian captivity of the Northern Kingdom and the destruction of Jerusalem
- Names Bethlehem as the place of the Messiah's birth
- Message of future deliverance, a reminder of God's promises to Abraham and Israel

Content Highlights:
- God's judgment on Judah, Samaria, and false Prophets
- God's judgment on the leaders
- Promise of deliverance and restoration

KEY VERSES & NOTES

And what doth the Lord require of thee, but to do justly, and to love mercy, and to walk humbly with thy God?
Micah 6:8b KJV

KEY VERSES

- 1:2, 5
- 2:3
- 2:12-13
- 3:4
- 3:9,12
- 4:1-5
- 5:2
- 5:8-9
- 6:6-8
- 6:13-16
- 7:7-9
- 7:18-20

KEY WORDS
Vision
Transgression
The Remnant of Jacob

THEME
God is gracious, merciful, and just.
God keeps His promises.

©2023 Wildrose Media

NAHUM

AUTHOR: Nahum, a prophet and poet.
SETTING: The Northern Kingdom has been conquered by Assyria.
TIME PERIOD: About 100 years after Jonah's ministry to Nineveh.
LITERARY STYLE: Poetry, Prophecy

The OLD TESTAMENT
BOOK # 34
3 CHAPTERS

Key People
Nahum
King of Assyria

Key Places
Nineveh
Judah
Jacob/Israel
Thebes
The Nile
Egypt

Key Events
The book of Nahum is a celebration of divine retribution, payback for the mistreatment of God's people by their enemies.

Content Highlights
- God's Power and Greatness Extolled
- Nineveh's Destruction Predicted
- The Destruction of Nineveh

KEY VERSES & NOTES

The Lord is slow to anger, and great in power; and will not at all acquit the wicked...
Nahum 1:3a KJV

KEY VERSES

- 1:2-3
- 1:6-7
- 1:12-13
- 1:15
- 2:13
- 3:1
- 3:18-19

KEY WORDS
Oracle
Vengeance
Woe
Exile

THEME
God is good and compassionate.
God will not let the guilty go unpunished.

©2023 Wildrose Media

HABAKKUK

AUTHOR: The prophet Habakkuk.
SETTING: In the southern kingdom of Judah.
TIME PERIOD: During the reign of King Josiah.
LITERARY STYLE: Prophecy, Poetry, a Song

The OLD TESTAMENT
BOOK # 35
3 CHAPTERS

Key People
Habakkuk
Babylonians

Key Places
Lebanon
Mount Paran
Midian

Key Events

General Information:
- Babylon is also known as Chaldea
- Habakkuk was a contemporary of Ezekiel, Daniel, Jeremiah and Zephaniah.

Questions from Habakkuk & Responses from God:
- Why Does God Permit Sin Among His People?
- God Responds
- Why Does God Allow the Unrighteous to Be Successful?
- God Responds
- Habakkuk's Prayer

KEY VERSES & NOTES

For the vision is yet for an appointed time, but at the end it shall speak and not lie: though it tarry, wait for it; because it will surely come, it will not tarry.
Habakkuk 2:3 KJV

KEY VERSES

- 1:2
- 1:5-6
- 1:13
- 2:8
- 2:14
- 2:18-20
- 3:2
- 3:17-19

KEY WORDS
Oracle
Judgment
Revelation
Righteous

THEME
No one can avoid God's discipline.

©2023 Wildrose Media

ZEPHANIAH

AUTHOR: Zephaniah (1:1), a descendant of King Hezekiah.
SETTING: In Judah during the beginning of Josiah's reign.
TIME PERIOD: Likely between 635 B.C.-625 B.C.
LITERARY STYLE: Poetry, Prophecy

The OLD TESTAMENT
BOOK # 36
3 CHAPTERS

Key People
- Zephaniah
- The Remnant
- The Nations
- The Kingdoms

Key Places
- Judah
- Jerusalem
- Israel
- Gaza
- Philistines
- Ashkelon
- Moab
- Ammon
- Nineveh
- Assyria
- "My Holy Hill"

Key Events
- Warning of Destruction
- The Judgment of Judah
- The Judgment of the Gentile Nations
- Jerusalem's Future
- Future Blessings for Jews and Gentiles

KEY VERSES & NOTES

*The Lord thy God
in the midst of thee
is mighty; he will save,
he will rejoice
over thee with joy...*
Zephaniah 3:17a KJV

KEY VERSES

- 1:4-6
- 1:13
- 1:14, 17-18
- 2:3
- 2:6-7
- 2:10-11
- 3:1-2
- 3:12-13
- 3:14-20

KEY WORDS
The Great Day of the Lord
Destroy, Demolish
Daughter of Zion
Rejoice

THEME
Rebellion against God must be punished.
Once cleansed, a remnant of Jews and Gentiles will be fully restored and once again receive God's blessing.

©2023 Wildrose Media

HAGGAI

AUTHOR: The prophet Haggai.
SETTING: Persian King Cyrus had allowed the Jews to return to Judah.
TIME PERIOD: The first exiles returned to Judah in 538 B.C.
LITERARY STYLE: Poetry, Prophecy

The OLD TESTAMENT
BOOK # 37
2 CHAPTERS

Key People
King Darius
Haggai
Zerubbabel
The Remnant
The Priests

Key Places
Judah
The Temple

Key Events

General Information:
- Haggai had seen the Temple before it was destroyed by Nebuchadnezzar in 586 B.C.
- He was about 70 years old when he ministered to the people.

Content Highlights:
- A Call to Judah to 'Consider Their Ways'
- A Call to Rebuild the Temple
- God Declares His Glory Will Return to the Temple
- Blessings
- God's Message to Zerubbabel

KEY VERSES & NOTES

Thus saith the Lord of hosts; consider your ways.
    Haggai 1:7 KJV

KEY VERSES

- 1:7
- 1:9-10
- 1:12
- 2:5
- 2:6-9

KEY WORDS
The Lord's House
Message

THEME
God delights in obedience.

©2023 Wildrose Media

ZECHARIAH

AUTHOR: Zechariah, a prophet and priest.
SETTING: In Judah, Zechariah was among the first to return to Judah.
TIME PERIOD: Likely between 538 B.C.-515 B.C., while Temple is rebuilt.
LITERARY STYLE: Poetry, Prophecy

The OLD TESTAMENT
BOOK # 38
14 CHAPTERS

Key People
Darius
Zechariah
Joshua
The Flock
The Clans & Wives

Key Places
Judah
Jerusalem
Ephraim
Mount of Olives

Key Events
General Information:
Contains several prophesies about the coming Messiah.
- Zechariah gives words of encouragement to the Jews.

Preface
The book is broken into 3 sections.
1. The Eight Visions (ch 1-6)
2. The Four Messages (ch 8 & 9)
3. The Two Oracles (ch 9-14)

KEY VERSES & NOTES

"Turn ye unto me, saith the Lord of hosts, and I will turn unto you saith the Lord of hosts".
Zechariah 1:3b KJV

KEY VERSES

- 1:3, 17
- 2:10-11
- 5:5-11
- 7:8-14
- 8:6-8
- 9:9
- 10:6
- 11:7-17
- 13:7-9

KEY WORDS
Forefathers
The Word of the Lord
Sheep/The Flock
Shepherd
Cleanse
Holy

THEME
God is faithful to His covenant promises.

©2023 Wildrose Media

MALACHI

AUTHOR: Most scholars agree on Malachi, some give Ezra or Mordecai credit.
SETTING: Temple priests & the people were violating God's laws.
TIME PERIOD: About 100 years since the Jewish exiles had returned to Judah.
LITERARY STYLE: Q & A, Prophetic Oracles

The OLD TESTAMENT
BOOK # 39
4 CHAPTERS

Key People
Jacob (Israel)
Esau (Edom)
Priests
The Righteous
The Wicked
Moses

Key Places
Israel
Edom
Judah
Jerusalem
Mount Horeb

Key Events
General Information:
- Malachi is the last of the minor prophets
- It is the final BOOK of the Old Testament, there are about 400 years of silence before events in the New Testament occur.

Summary:
- Chapter 1 God's Love for His People
- Chapter 1-2 The Disrespect and Improper Worship of the Priests
- Chapter 2-3 The Unfaithfulness of the People
- Chapter 3-4 Hope for Israel's Future
- Chapter 4 The Day of the Lord

KEY VERSES & NOTES

Behold, I will send my messenger, and he shall prepare the way before me: and the LORD, whom ye seek, shall suddenly come to his temple, even the messenger of the covenant, whom ye delight in: behold, he shall come, saith the LORD of hosts.
Malachi 3:1 KJV

KEY VERSES

- 1:2-5
- 1:11, 14
- 2:7-9
- 3:2-5
- 3:6-7
- 3:16-17
- 4:1, 5-6

KEY WORDS
Love and Hate
Defiled – Contemptible - Wrath
Blessings and Curses
Messenger of the Covenant
The Day of the Lord

THEME
God loves His people and will deliver them as He promised.

©2023 Wildrose Media

Wildrose Media website
- Home - Page

Faith Family Fun Blog
Homeschool Tips +

Wildrose Media website
- Shop - Page

Additional books from Wildrose Media, available on Amazon:

Sermon Notebook
Kids Ages 9-12 years
Cross cover

Sermon Notebook
Kids Ages 6-8 years
Bunny cover

The Birth of Jesus
Coloring Book

The Story of Easter
Coloring Book
Blue cover

Bible Teaching Sheets
Old TESTAMENT - KJV

Bible Teaching Sheets
New TESTAMENT - KJV

Friendship and Freedom
Story of the Statue of Liberty

100 Questions to Ask Myself
Vol.1 - pink cover

Ultimate Fishing Journal
for Kids Vol. 1

Ultimate Fishing Journal
for Girls - pink cover

Headache Diary, 5"x 6"
Symptom Notebook

Dutch Boy & Girl
Small Notebook 5"x6"

The above BOOK QR codes are Amazon Affiliate links,
I may receive compensation from purchases made using these links,
at no additional cost to you.

Made in the USA
Las Vegas, NV
18 November 2023

81084913R00049